Book

Helping Others

by Mary Lindeen

NORWOOD HOUSE PRESS

DEAR CAREGIVER,

The *Beginning to Read—Read and Discover* books provide emergent readers the opportunity to explore the world through nonfiction while building early reading skills. The text integrates both common sight words and content vocabulary. These key words are featured on lists provided at the back of the book to help your child expand his or her sight word recognition, which helps build reading fluency. The content words expand vocabulary and support comprehension.

Nonfiction text is any text that is factual. The Common Core State Standards call for an increase in the amount of informational text reading among students. The Standards aim to promote college and career readiness among students. Preparation for college and career endeavors requires proficiency in reading complex informational texts in a variety of content areas. You can help your child build a foundation by introducing nonfiction early. To further support the CCSS, you will find Reading Reinforcement activities at the back of the book that are aligned to these Standards.

Above all, the most important part of the reading experience is to have fun and enjoy it!

Sincerely,

Shannon Cannon

Shannon Cannon, Ph.D.
Literacy Consultant

Norwood House Press • P.O. Box 316598 • Chicago, Illinois 60631
For more information about Norwood House Press please visit our website at
www.norwoodhousepress.com or call 866-565-2900.
© 2016 Norwood House Press. Beginning-to-Read™ is a trademark of Norwood House Press.
All rights reserved. No part of this book may be reproduced or utilized in any form or by any
means without written permission from the publisher.

Editor: Judy Kentor Schmauss
Designer: Lindaanne Donohoe

Photo Credits:

Shutterstock, cover, 1, 3, 4-5, 10, 11, 12-13, 16, 17, 18-19, 24-25; Dreamstime, 8-9
(© Elenathewise), 14-15 (© Photographerlondon), 22-23 (© Jarenwicklund); iStock, 20-21;
Phil Martin, 6-7, 26-27, 28-29

Library of Congress Cataloging-in-Publication Data
  Lindeen, Mary.
  Helping others / by Mary Lindeen.
      pages cm. – (A beginning to read book)
  Summary: "There are many ways to be a good helper. You can help at home, at school,
on the bus, and outside. You can also ask for help when you need it. It feels good to help
others. This title includes reading activities and a word list"– Provided by publisher.
  ISBN 978-1-59953-700-9 (library edition : alk. paper)
  ISBN 978-1-60357-785-4 (ebook)
  1. Helping behavior in children–Juvenile literature. I. Title.
  BF723.H45L56 2015
  177'.7–dc23
                                                                  2015001272

Manufactured in the United States of America in Stevens Point, Wisconsin. 275N-062015

How can you be a good helper?
There are many things you can do
to help others.
You can be a big help all day long!

You can help in the morning.

You can make your bed.

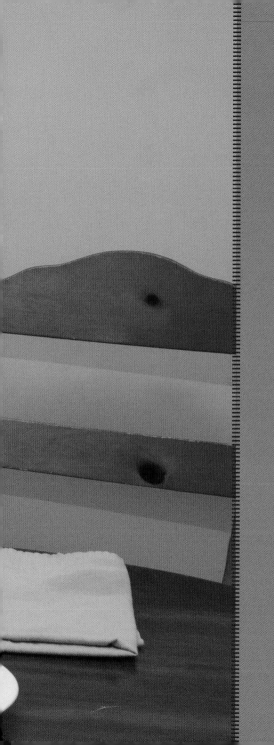

You can set the table.

Please get the spoons and bowls.

You can help at school.

You can hold the door.

Thank you!

You can help the teacher.

You can get the books.

You can work
quietly.

This helps everyone
learn better.

You can help on the bus.

You can wait your turn.

This helps the driver.

You can help after school.
You can get your own snack.

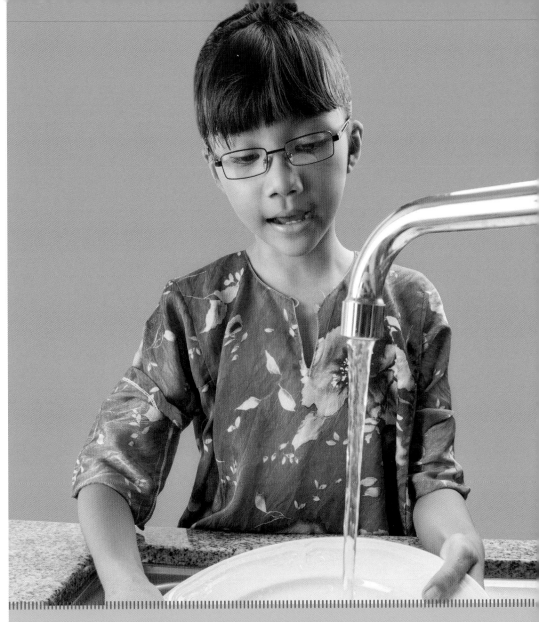

Remember to clean up
when you are done!

You can help outside.

You can walk the dog.

You can pull the weeds.

That will help the flowers grow.

You can help
someone you love.

You can help him
feel very happy!

You can help at night.

You can put your toys away.

This will help your family.

You can ask for help, too.

It is okay to ask someone to help you.

You helped a lot
of people today.

Thank you!

...READING REINFORCEMENT...

CRAFT AND STRUCTURE

To check your child's understanding of this book, recreate the following diagram on a sheet of paper. Read the book with your child, and then help him or her fill in the diagram using what they learned. Work together to identify words, facts, and ideas related to helping others.

Helping Others

VOCABULARY: Learning Content Words

Content words are words that are specific to a particular topic. All of the content words for this book can be found on page 32. Use some or all of these content words to complete one or more of the following activities:

- Ask your child to use his or her own words to define each of the content words. Have your child use each content word in a sentence.

- Name one or two attributes of a content word without saying the word; for example, This is made of paper and has words and pictures in it. (book) Have your child guess the word. Switch roles.

- Say a content word. Have your child say the first word that comes to his or her mind. Discuss connections between the two words.

- Say a content word and have your child act out its meaning.

- Ask your child to sort the content words into two, three, or four categories of their own choosing. Then have him or her explain what the words in each category have in common.

FOUNDATIONAL SKILLS: Nouns

Nouns are words that name people, places, things, or ideas. Have your child identify which words are nouns in the list below. Then help your child find nouns in this book.

bed/better	okay/dog	thank/toys
bus/done	eat/spoons	weeds/pull
grow/flowers	teacher/learn	clean/table

CLOSE READING OF NONFICTION TEXT

Close reading helps children comprehend text. It includes reading a text, discussing it with others, and answering questions about it. Use these questions to discuss this book with your child:

• What are three things you can do to help other people?

• What is the difference between helping at home and helping at school?

• What are some other ways of helping that were not mentioned in the book?

• Why is getting your own snack helpful?

• How can you get someone to help you?

• Are you a helpful person? Why or why not?

FLUENCY

Fluency is the ability to read accurately with speed and expression. Help your child practice fluency by using one or more of the following activities:

• Reread this book to your child at least two times while he or she uses a finger to track each word as you read it.

• Read the first sentence aloud. Then have your child reread the sentence with you. Continue until you have finished this book.

• Ask your child to read aloud the words they know on each page of this book. (Your child will learn additional words with subsequent readings.)

• Have your child practice reading this book several times to improve accuracy, rate, and expression.

••• Word List •••

Helping Others uses the 82 vocabulary words listed below. *High-frequency* words are those words that are used most often in the English language. They are sometimes referred to as sight words because children need to learn to recognize them automatically when they read. *Content words* are any words specific to a particular topic. Regular practice reading these words will enhance your child's ability to read with greater fluency and comprehension.

High-Frequency Words

a	big	in	people	to
after	can	is	put	up
all	day	it	school	very
and	do	long	set	when
are	get	make	that	will
ask	good	many	the	work
at	help(ed, er, s)	on	there	you
away	him	other(s)	things	your
be	how	own	this	

Content Words

bed	door	learn	quietly	today
better	driver	lot	remember	toys
books	everyone	love	snack	turn
bowls	family	morning	someone	wait
bus	feel	night	spoons	walk
clean	grow	outside	table	weeds
dog	happy	please	teacher	
done	hold	pull	thank	

••• About the Author

Mary Lindeen is a writer, editor, parent, and former elementary school teacher. She has written more than 100 books for children and edited many more. She specializes in early literacy instruction and books for young readers, especially nonfiction.

••• About the Advisor

Dr. Shannon Cannon is a teacher educator in the School of Education at UC Davis, where she also earned her Ph.D. in Language, Literacy, and Culture. She serves on the clinical faculty, supervising pre-service teachers and teaching elementary methods courses in reading, effective teaching, and teacher action research.